ODD DOGS

CHAIRMAN OF THE BOARD
SHEBASCO PET FOODS INC.

SIMON BOND

ODD DOGS

A hundred and one scenes of canine life

PERENNIAL LIBRARY

Harper & Row, Publishers, New York
Grand Rapids, Philadelphia, St. Louis, San Francisco
London, Singapore, Sydney, Tokyo, Toronto

First PERENNIAL LIBRARY edition published
1990.

LIBRARY OF CONGRESS CATALOG CARD NUMBER
89-45871

ISBN 0-06-096485-5

90 91 92 93 94 RRD 10 9 8 7 6 5 4 3 2 1

'Oh my God, dog biscuits are down!'

'And in lane four, representing Battersea Dogs Home ...'

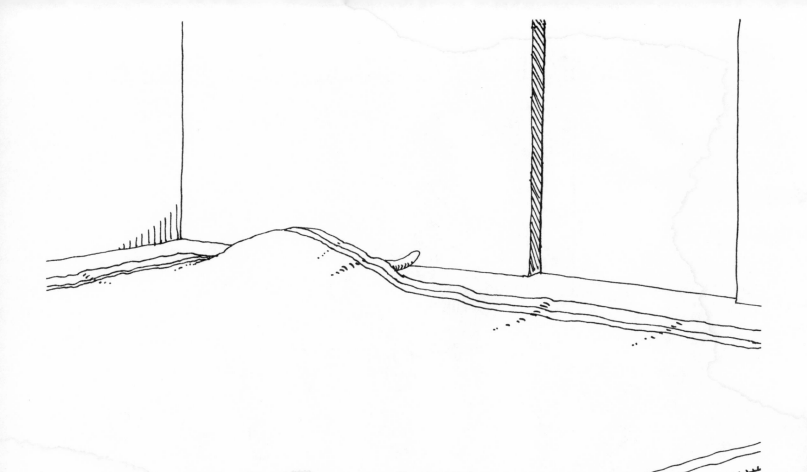

THE WORD BATH IS MENTIONED

BEYOND THE CALL OF DUTY

'Oh yes, occasionally he's very boisterous.'

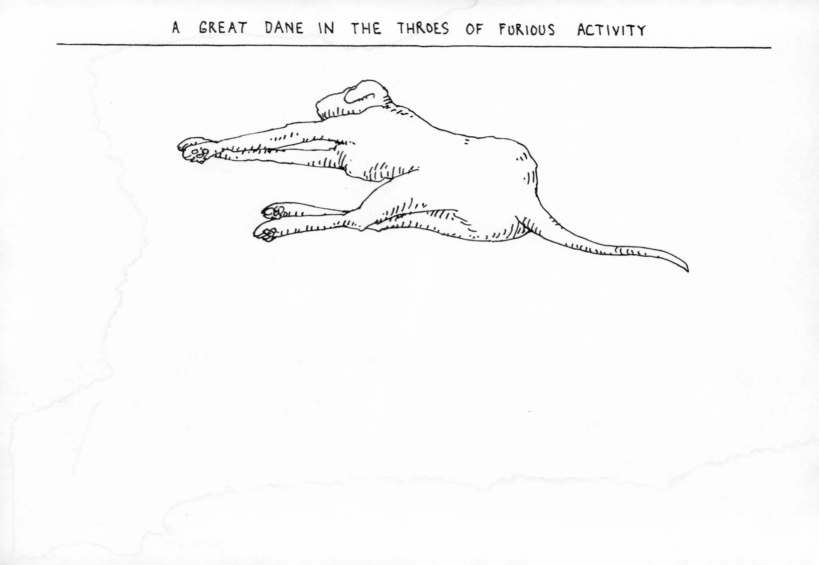

THE LONE RANGER
AND FIDO

'Forget it . . . just black coffee'

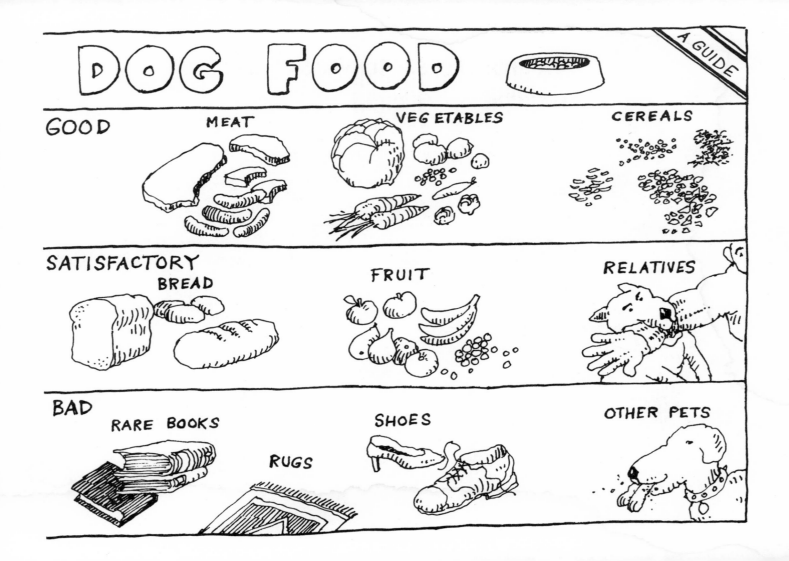

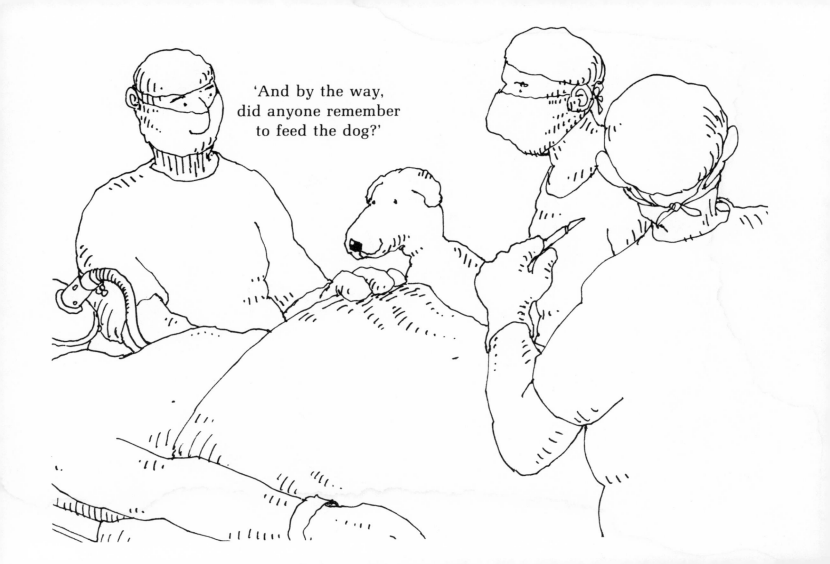

KNOW YOUR DOG

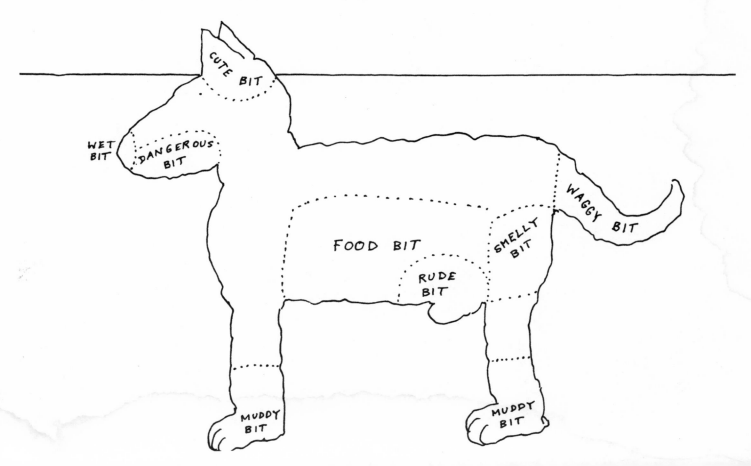

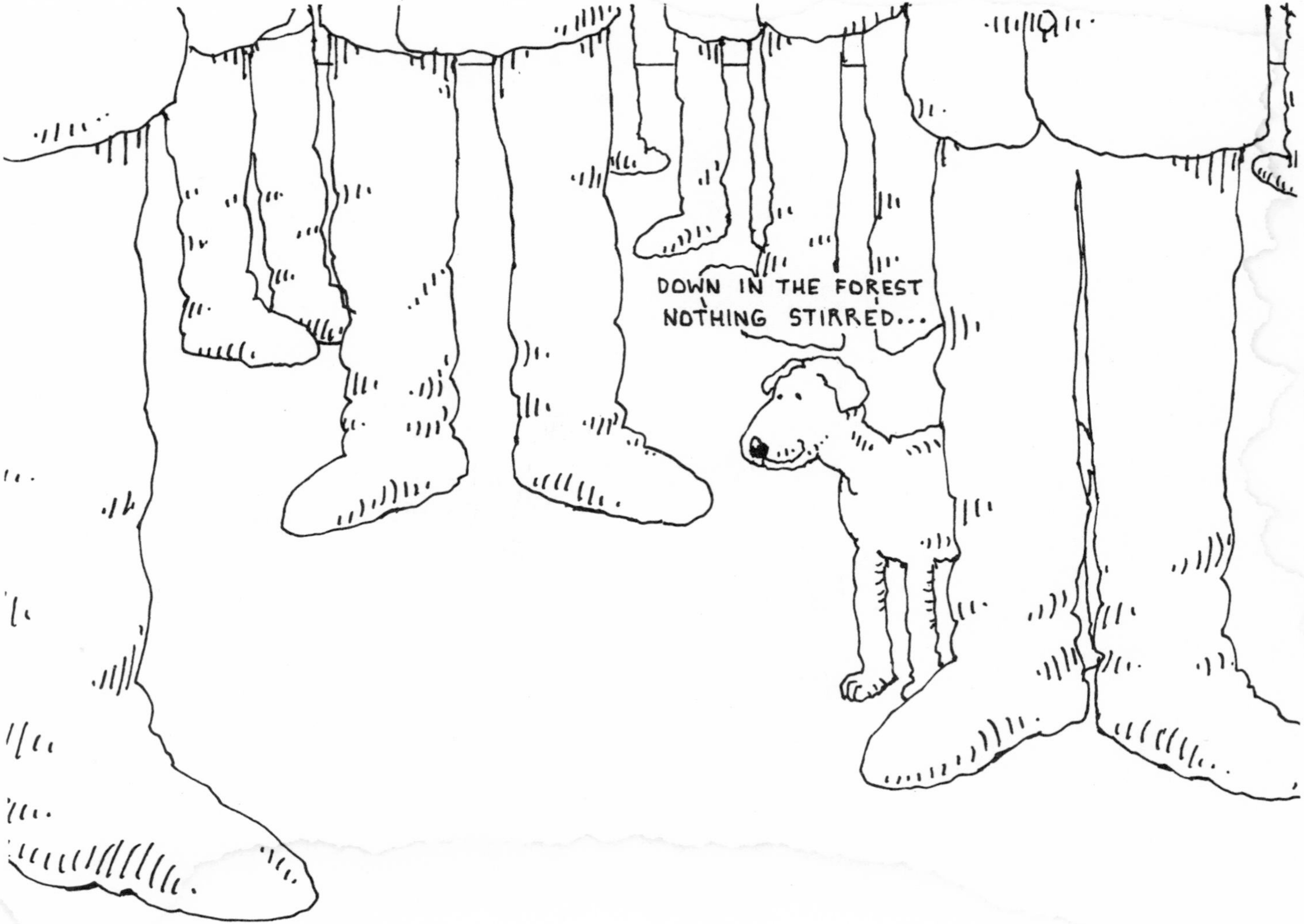
DOWN IN THE FOREST
NOTHING STIRRED...

'Lord and Lady
Lascelles de Vere Digby
and their ratty
little mongrel, Tinker.'

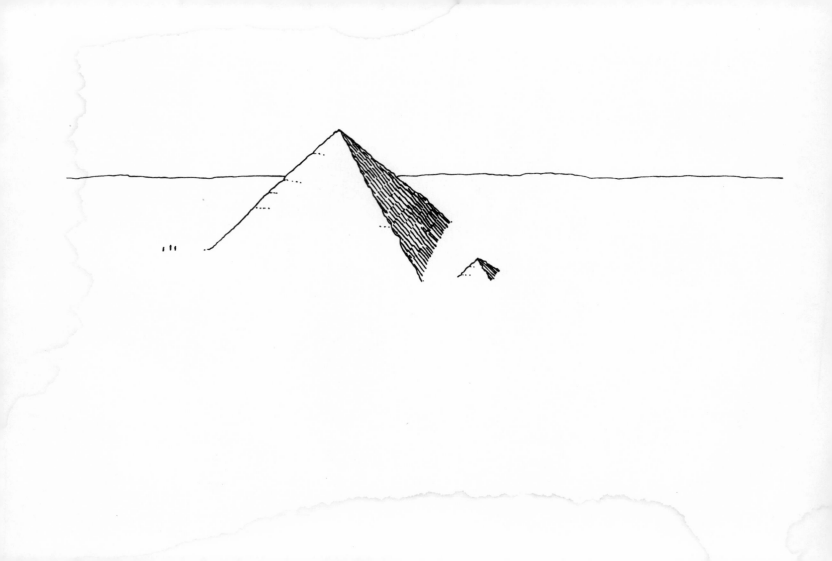

'Oh Rex, can we really afford it?'

'Singing and dancing no problem ... but I don't do nude scenes.'

'Margie, this dog's got to go . . . he's just too cute!'

THE FIRST MESS

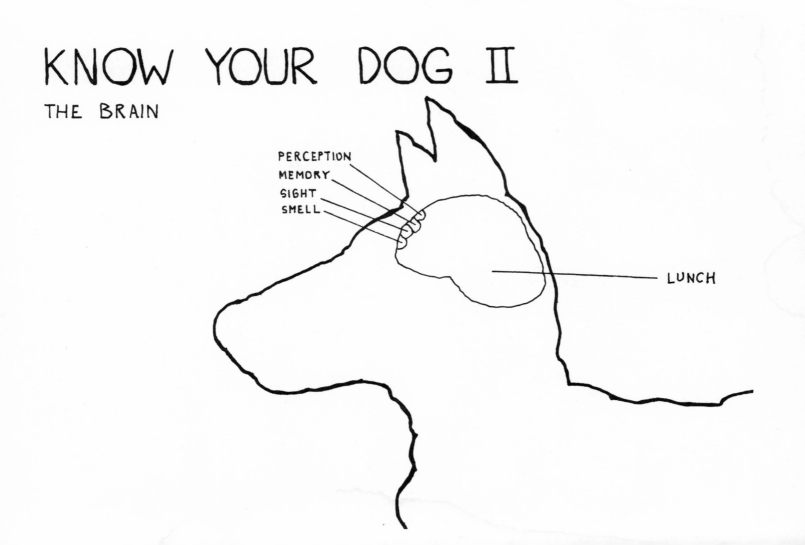

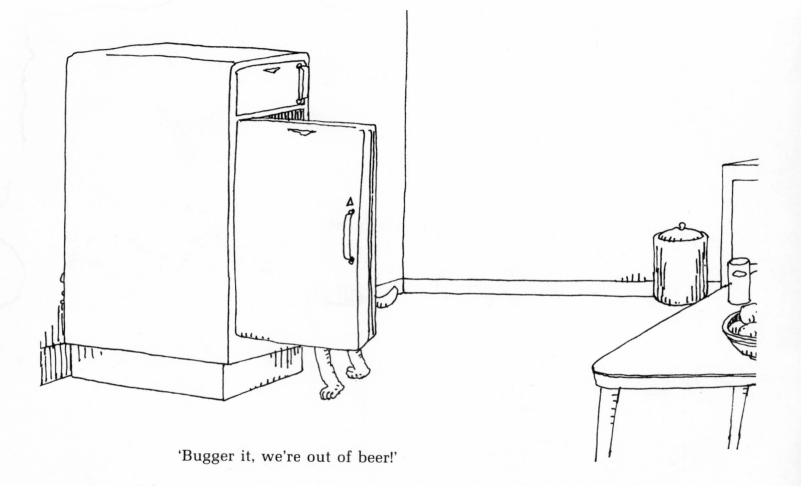

'Bugger it, we're out of beer!'

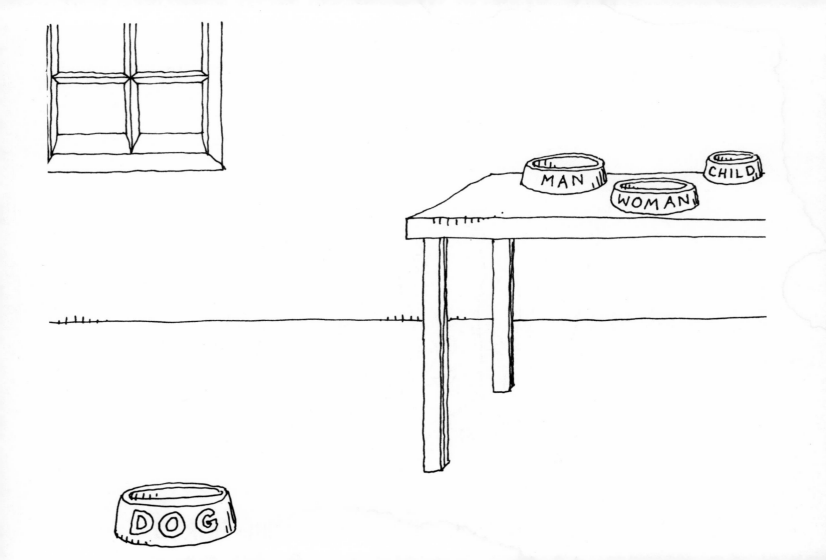

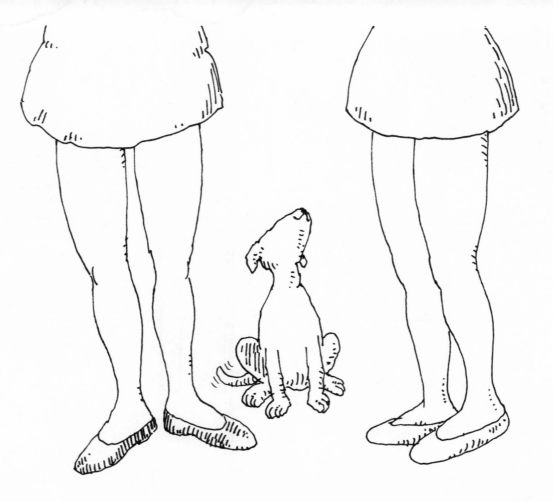

SCOTTY—THE DOG WHO LOVED MINI-SKIRTS

'Oh yes, he's wonderfully obedient.'

'And who ordered the dry martini with a dash of liver?'

'Katherine, why can't he eat like other dogs?'

'Sorry to bother you Mr Hellerman,
but do you think you could just
pop in and change the channel?'

'Are you stupid – it's pouring down!'

'Alice, apparently I'm taking King for a walk.'

'Well, if a dog's going to beg, that's the way to do it.'

'And when you want
to go to the toilet
would you please bark.'

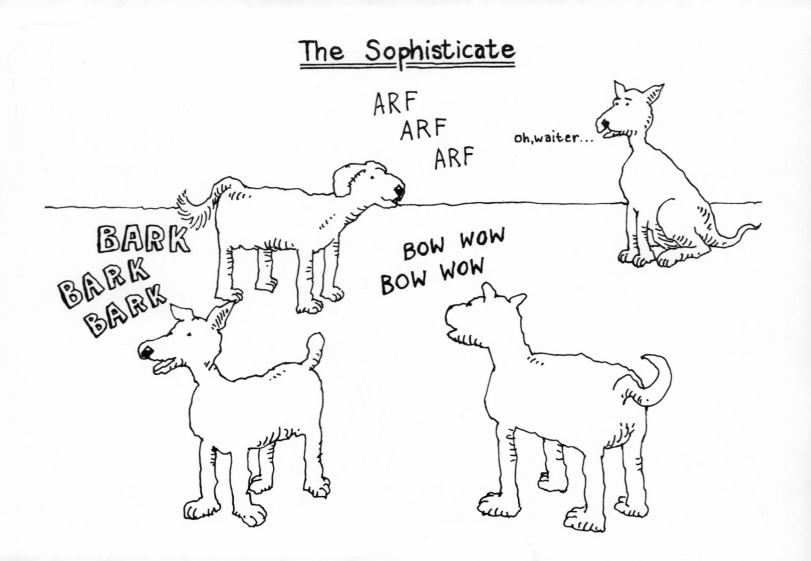

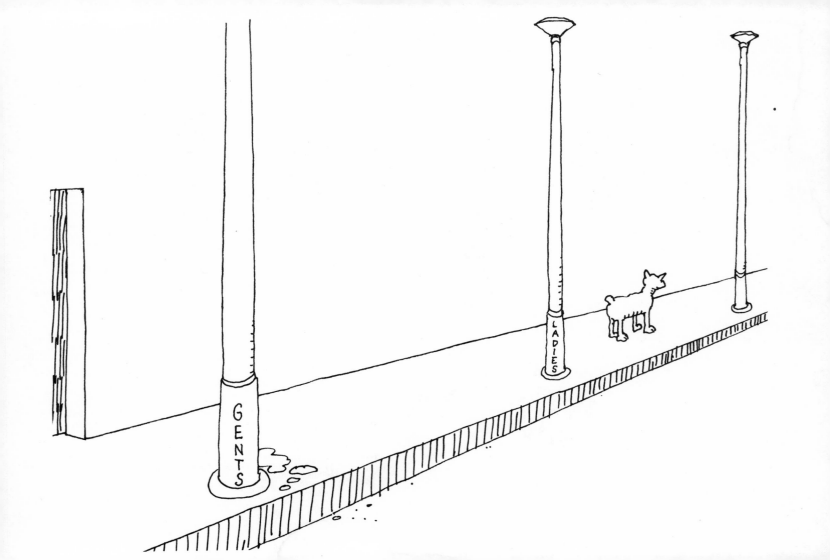

THE HOUND OF THE BASKETBALLS

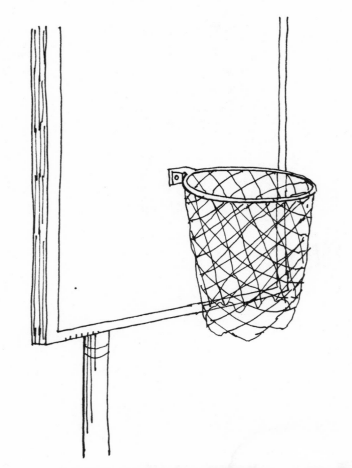
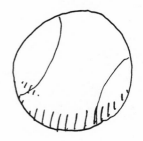

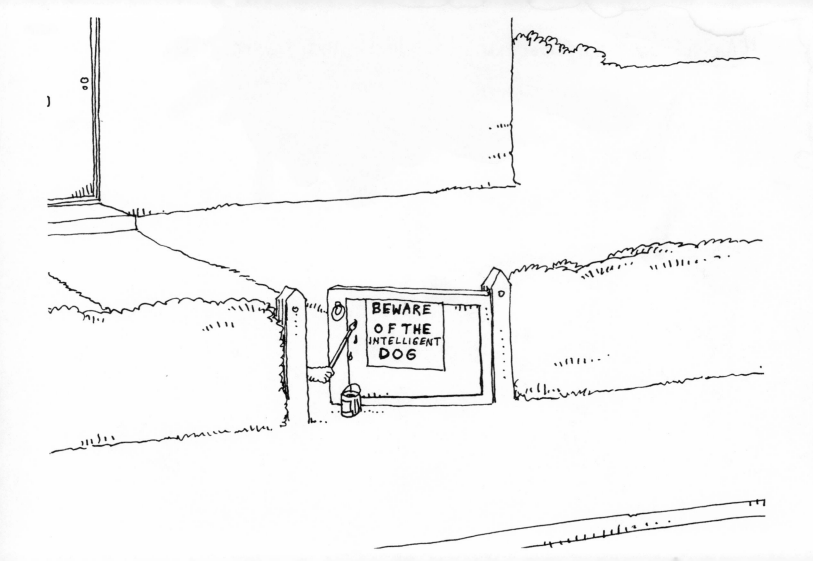

MAY 1939   The Germans Invade Poland (Surreptitiously)

'Well, I thought the water
to wine bit was nice,
now how about some new legs?'

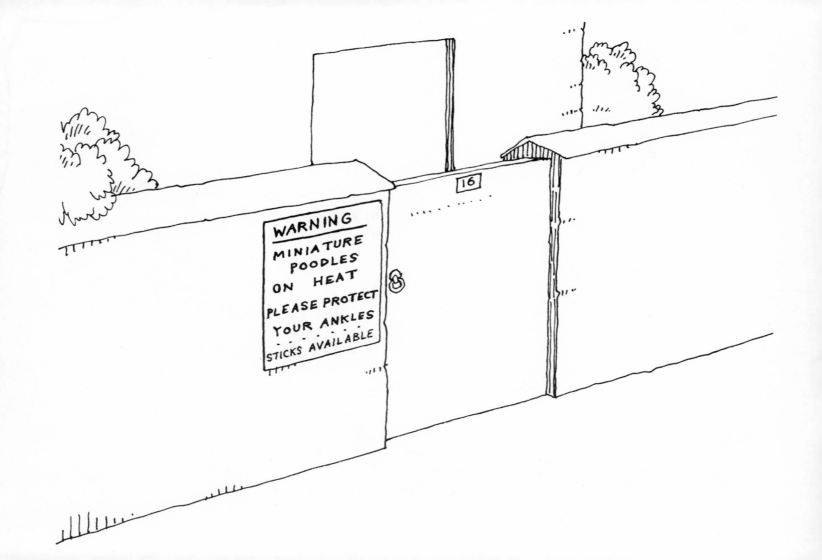

'If he misses, can I have the apple?'

'Macready, there's someone at the front door . . . attack them and bring me their wallet.'

The mighty warrior Vlaric surveyed the open plain... his muscled torso ready for battle...
And at his side his majestic hound Druce sat patiently waiting........

IRONY

'Jesus! I thought mine was bad.'

'Just where the hell have you been, I've been worried sick!'

THE TUTANKHAMEN EXPEDITION 1908 (The Economy Version)

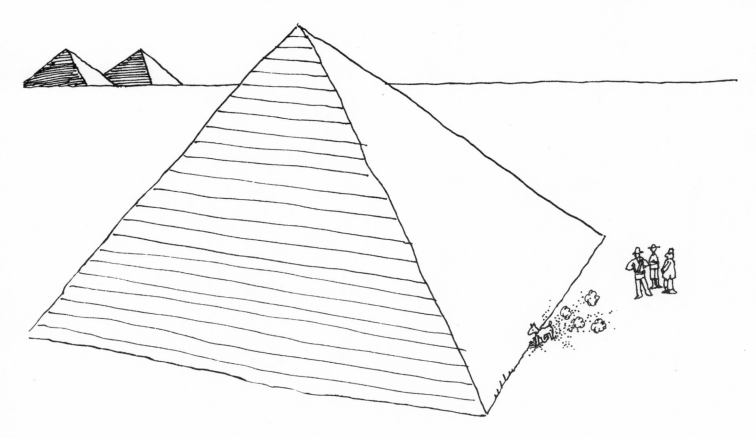

'Rusty, do it like everyone else, will you!'

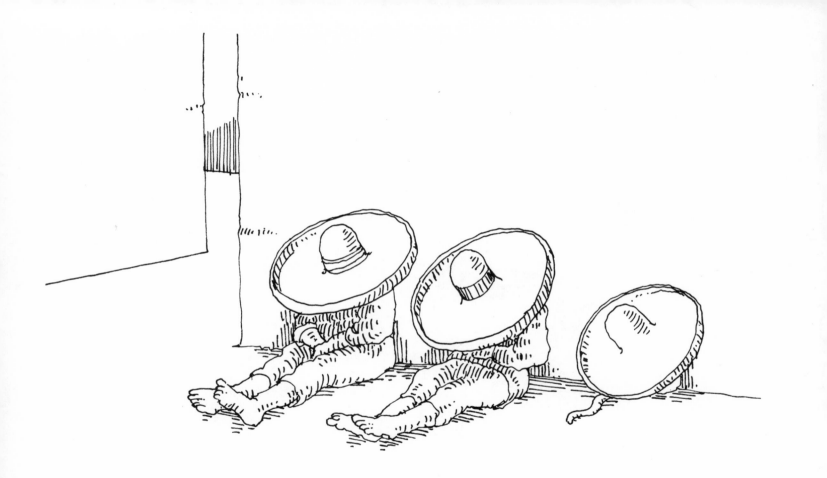

'Forgive me father,
for I have sinned . . .
I ate a paperback and
pee-ed on the carpet.'

'Four across is "Carpathian" ...'

'And when did you last see our supper?'

THE NINTH WONDER
OF THE WORLD

THE GREAT MONGREL
OF MANCHU

SIT !

NOW WE'VE FINISHED
THIS BOOK YOU KNOW
WHAT WE SHOULD DO.

                NO WHAT?

WE SHOULD GO AND NOSE
AROUND SOME GARBAGE.

                OH YES LET'S.